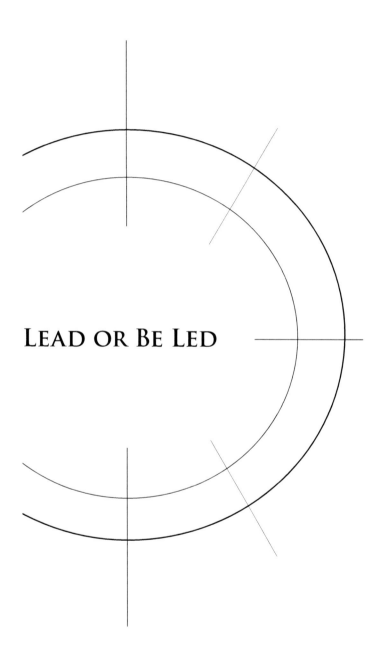

LEAD OR BE LED

Having devoted myself to the lessons and actions set forth in these pages, I now live my life pro-actively, with happiness at every turn. So get ready to enjoy all the energy and passion that comes with choosing your path. It is a wonderful way to live!

Michael Magura
Managing Director, South Asia
Intransa Inc.

Lead or Be Led is a blueprint for increasing personal value. Bill Munn's words provide us with the tools to take charge of our future and strengthen our own authenticity. Reading this book will impact your own life as well as the lives of everyone you touch.

Joan Durgin
Coordinator, Health Services
Toledo Public Schools

I have worked with Bill for years and have benefited from his insights on both a personal and professional level. This book is the next-best thing to a coaching session with the author. He brings his concepts to light with colorful examples and outlines the implementation tools that will move us closer to our goals.

Tony Kalich
Regional Director
DIAGEO-Guinness USA

Bill Munn does not tell us how to live, but brings the learning to his readers so that we might make it our own. In this way, he expertly teaches us that a life (like a school or any other organization) is a breathing, changing organism in which goals and visions must be constantly re-visited, assessed, and refined.

Sue Fuller
School Principal

Lead or Be Led is a decadent slice of fudge in a world of vanilla books. It's so rich with wisdom that you'll miss out if you try to gobble it up too quickly. Savor and enjoy!

Don Fothergill
Pastor

Do you have trouble prioritizing at school or in the work place? Do you struggle to manage your daily affairs or achieve personal objectives in a timely manner? If you can relate, read this book! *Lead or Be Led* is the pathway to your peace of mind.

Casey Cortez
College Student

Lead or Be Led is a great resource for learning to manage, organize, and execute life. It's practical at any age and in any vocation. A book you should read every year!

Amanda Greene
Homemaker and Mother

LEAD OR BE LED
A GUIDE FOR INTENTIONAL LIVING

BY
BILL MUNN

Wordclay
1663 Liberty Drive, Suite 200
Bloomington, IN 47403
Phone: 1-800-839-8640

First published by Wordclay 11/17/2008

ISBN: 978-1-6048-1393-7 (sc)
ISBN: 978-1-6048-1266-4 (dj)

Library of Congress Number: 2006930141

Printed in the United States of America
Bloomington, Indiana

This book is printed on acid-free paper.

For Lindy, my soul mate and wife, and my three girls, Wendy, Melissa, and Libby. There but for the grace of you goes an unintentional guy.

"The purpose of life is a life of purpose."
—Robert Byrne

"Happiness is not a destination. It is a method of life."
—Burton Hills

THE TRIP

"What went wrong?" Ted whispered. He'd been talking to himself a lot ever since conversations with Carol had become more depressing.

She slept in the passenger seat as he drove across the endless Kansas flatlands toward home. The gray sky matched his feelings. He felt an empty pit inside, and something was pulling him into it.

Ted's mind returned to the beginning. Years ago, while he and Carol were engaged, they talked about the future and the goals they had. And what a list it was! Almost everything they admired in other people's lives was added to their plans: travel, careers, finances, children, home, neighborhood, even retirement. Back then, everything seemed so achievable. And there was so much time. Yet now, the "what went wrong" column seemed longer than that old list of dreams.

At that moment, Ted was struck with a sad analogy. Their lives had turned out like this trip—many plans followed by few results. But why?

Just then, he was snapped from daydreaming by Carol's voice. "Where are we?" she yawned.

"Kansas," he reported.

"Still?! This state must last forever."

"Five thousand miles," he quipped sarcastically.

Silence returned for a while. Then Carol asked, "Where's your mind?"

"I don't know … I guess I was just thinking that our life is a lot like this trip. A mismatch between goals and results."

"Yeah, so do you just enjoy negative thoughts?"

He ignored this and continued. "Think about it. We were excited to visit the West Coast. We saved up our money and vacation time. We talked about all the places we'd visit. Then we didn't even get there. We had to turn around in Utah."

"The story of our life," Carol summarized.

"That's my point."

"Okay, let's look at what happened." Carol straightened in her seat as she warmed to the topic. "We lost a week in nowhere, Ohio, while waiting for a fuel pump because Mr. Conceptual didn't have the car serviced before we left. Then we got lost seven times when Mr. Macho wouldn't ask for directions. Finally, we wasted all that time dropping in on your college buddies. Add that up and we at least would have seen a portion of the West Coast."

"Look, if it helps you to blame me, then go ahead. But you're ignoring all the extra days spent on your love affair with outlet malls. Do you want to count those?"

"No." Now Carol wanted to change the subject. "But deducting all those delays still doesn't account for missing our schedule by a whole month. A bigger issue was the stuff we couldn't predict."

"Like?"

"Like four huge construction delays. Like your boss ordering you back to the office. And who knew the Pennsylvania Highway Patrol considers their speed limit a sacred law? We could have made it if all those unexpected details hadn't gotten in the way."

Ted enjoyed not being the target of fault. "Yeah," he agreed. "And look at all the silly errands we ran for people back home, and the side trips our friends recommended that proved useless in the end."

"You know, you're right, honey!" Carol exclaimed.

Hmm, when was the last time she'd said "honey"? He was feeling better than he had in days.

The positive atmosphere grew as she continued. "I know how we fix this next time. As soon as you get that promotion, we'll have more money and more vacation time. Then we'll fly to the coast. With the bucks and the time, our problems will be solved."

"Good idea," he enthused. "In fact, when I played golf with Tom, I was newly convinced that we should go into business for ourselves. He's got so much freedom and all the money he needs. Plus, we could live anywhere we like."

With the subject of their failed journey pushed aside, Ted and Carol began discussing future dreams, and they both felt much better by the time they finally arrived at home.

Later, as Carol slept beside him in the comfort of their own bed, Ted's mind was momentarily troubled. He suddenly remembered his thought in Kansas: Their lives had turned out like this trip—many plans followed by few results. But why? That essential question still had not been answered.

But the memory soon faded and sleep took over.

"What you do speaks so loudly that I cannot hear what you say."
—Ralph Waldo Emerson

CHAPTER 1

ONLY THREE LIVES CHANGED

Picture yourself in the bookstore looking at a title in the Self Help or Management section which states triumphantly "8 MILLION COPIES SOLD." You would probably be impressed.

But what if you read "8 MILLION COPIES SOLD (but only 3 lives changed)"? Your reaction would be less enthusiastic. In fact, this is often the case. We do a seminar. We read a book. When we're finished, we say, "GREAT! That's really good stuff!" Then we go home and return to our daily lives. By next Wednesday, we are operating exactly the same way as before. How does this happen? Why do we not change our day-to-day lives to reflect the material that so impressed us?

The answer lies in implementation tools. We need specific next steps— steps we can take today to start us toward our goals. Like Ted and Carol, we find the challenge not in the big picture, but in the details of taking action. In this book, you will find both the necessary tools to create your own plan and the methods you can use in your day-to-day life to make that plan succeed. These methods are described as "implementation tools."

An analogy might be helpful. Let's say you are devoted to physical exercise. Your friend, whom you care about, is your opposite. She is overweight and totally without any workout experience. You finally talk her into an exercise session. Would you start the first day off with a ten-mile run? I doubt it. If you did, she would probably get seriously injured. At minimum, she would be discouraged from any further effort.

More likely, you would design some start-up exercises for your friend. You might begin by convincing her to walk around the block. Later, you might suggest a longer walk, then a little jogging, and finally some longer distances. This process of immediate but small steps, if continued over time, would lead to a major improvement in her physical condition.

The implementation exercises in this book are designed to offer you baby steps so you don't have to start with a ten-mile run at the very beginning of your journey.

I heard a story about a young Illinois Agricultural Department employee who was assigned to promote a new planting technology to farmers. He was really excited about this development and what it could mean to productivity. When he visited his first farmer, he explained this new process with great enthusiasm. His listener responded, "Son, I'm already not farming as well as I know how."

We can learn from this farmer. We know how to do it better. The issue we struggle with is actually doing something with our knowledge. Consider the example with your friend exercising. She knows about working out, but she doesn't do it. Many of us know what we want to change, but if we don't live intentionally, we lack the tools that will help us achieve any lasting transformation in our lives.

Every year on January 1st, millions of people resolve to make changes in their lives, yet so few achieve their goals that the concept of New Year's resolutions has virtually become a worldwide joke. We list our dreams lazily, as if we can take a magic pill to make them all come true. But we must be intentional in every effort and active in every step on the journey through a life of purpose.

"Do not go where the path may lead. Go instead
where there is no path and leave a trail."
—Ralph Waldo Emerson

CHAPTER 2

LEAD OR BE LED

For twenty years, I have addressed the subject of intentional living in seminars, speaking engagements, and individual coaching sessions. It's interesting to hear participants respond to Ted and Carol's behavior during "The Trip." Many people offer judgmental feedback at first, but grow in understanding as they recognize the similarities between their own lives and the story of this discouraged couple.

Our travelers blamed one another, then circumstances, and finally other people in an attempt to convince themselves that everything would turn out better next time. They missed the point that their failure was due to lack of planning and focused implementation—in short, a lack of intentionality.

But before we treat Ted and Carol too harshly, let's peer into our own experience and ask why so many of us lead our lives the same way this couple managed their journey. Are we reproducing their mistakes? Sadly, for many of us, the answer is yes.

People use phrases that refer to "leading life." Some examples: "I want to lead a life that results in …" or "I hope people see that I have led a life of …"

The fact is that most people don't lead their lives. More often, life leads them. Like Ted and Carol, they take one exit ramp at a time. Then they wonder why the end result is not what they planned.

I respect the honesty and self-awareness with which people react to Ted and Carol's story. For example:

"I know I should plan, but I don't know how to start."

"Yeah, I have some goals, but I get distracted too—like Ted and Carol jumping on exit ramps."

"Frankly, I'm just going as fast as I can and hoping it all works out."

"How can I think long term? It's all I can do to get through each day."

"As soon as I make more money, everything will be fine."

If I had tape recordings of all my past sessions, this list would go on for pages. The point is, many people know at a conceptual level that a plan is important. However, they don't know how to start the process and/or they can't integrate it into their day-to-day living, so the plan exists as a road map that's irrelevant since nobody's traveling the route.

Incidentally, there is an objection several seminar participants have made at this point in our discussion: "I want to be spontaneous, live for today, and not worry about tomorrow."

Well, this may surprise you, but we are in agreement! Spontaneity adds spice to the meal of life. When you lead your life on purpose, you'll gain the ability to enjoy surprise "exit ramps" without allowing them to pull you off track.

We also agree on not worrying about tomorrow (or, for that matter, yesterday). Our subject is living on purpose, not worrying. Don't confuse the two. In fact, it is intentionality that eliminates worry. Ted and Carol worried about their life because of repeated mismatches between goals and results. Confidence in both their plan and their implementation ability would have mitigated that.

> "The road of life is paved with flat squirrels who
> couldn't decide which way to go."
> —Anonymous

CHAPTER 3

MEET YOUR ENEMY

You have a powerful enemy resisting your efforts to lead an intentional life. This vicious adversary goes by the name AS SOON AS. He has an equally deadly sister named IF ONLY. Together they will try to convince you that everything will be fine in your life as soon as (and if only) you:

- Get a promotion
- Move into a bigger house
- Find a new spouse
- Come up with a great business idea
- Get a new job
- The list goes on.

I have watched this brother-sister act hold many people hostage. They convince you that life is just a passive endeavor, so you don't need to do anything except wait. If (more commonly, when) hoped-for events don't happen, your opponent persuades you to simply blame it on circumstances beyond your control. AS SOON AS and IF ONLY keep you trapped in a cycle of hope followed by blame rather than one of purposeful action.

IMPLEMENTATION TOOL: DEFEAT YOUR ENEMY

First, attune yourself to its presence in your life. Listen to yourself. Notice each time you use phrases like "as soon as" or "if only." Ask someone close to you to point out the instances when you say these words.

Second, if you find these enemies seeping into your thinking, take action. Make an immediate note of at least one next step (no matter how small) that you are going to take now to make "as soon as" become reality.

Take action on this next small step today or tomorrow. Don't think about its significance when compared to the whole dream. That's not the point. The point is to turn your prior passive thoughts into action. This practice will gradually change your attitude from one of waiting to one of doing.

"The whole world steps aside for the man who knows where he is going."
—Anonymous

THE POWER OF
YOUR VISION

Because this term's popularity has led to its misuse, let's talk about what a vision is *not*. Many of you have seen plaques in business offices that read "Our Vision is ..." My rule is that if you moved that sign to any other organization and it still made sense to visitors, it is not an appropriate vision. The same principle applies to your personal life—your vision belongs to you alone. It is not a theoretical statement that could fit almost anyone.

It is typical for people to develop a vision that fits anywhere. "Be the best at what we do." "Be happy and successful." The list goes on. These examples sound good, but they aren't real or personal. Since they don't capture your dream, they don't ignite you and will not spark a change in your day-to-day behavior.

Most people misunderstand the power of the vision. Many think that it is a theoretical concept.

In reality, a well thought-through vision that you can relate to has extraordinary influence in guiding your day-to-day life. This happens because of the immense power of your subconscious compared to your conscious mind. Your conscious mind is okay at dealing with the task at hand and a few things you may be thinking about at the moment.

In contrast, your subconscious mind is capable of incredible complexity in interpreting and responding to the myriad of situations you face every day. This part of your brain can absorb and analyze mountains of input. As you repeatedly focus your conscious mind on your vision, the subconscious gradually incorporates this picture into its data bank. It then delivers to your conscious mind those decisions, judgments, and actions appropriate to accomplishing your future picture.

People often call this phenomenon an epiphany, insight, or intuition. In any case, it is both real and powerful, and can be learned as you focus on and internalize your vision.

To help you form a snapshot of your desired future situation, try the following fantasy. It's an exercise I call future-past thinking.

IMPLEMENTATION TOOL: FUTURE-PAST THINKING

First, pretend that you and I are meeting. I explain that I have gone into the future ten years, seen your life, and taken notes and photos. I have this information with me. As I open my briefcase to show you this material, what do you hope to see? What are your thoughts, hopes, and dreams? You can pause right now and visualize this. What is your picture? Write out a description of what you would like to see: "When Bill opens his briefcase, I hope he shows me …"

Be explicit and use descriptive language that helps you really internalize your image. Insert details like who is with you, what you are doing, how you are feeling, where you are, and other specifics that make it real. You can even note the sounds you hear or the smells in the air; the idea is to describe your vision in words that grab your heart.

Finally, post this word-picture in a place where you see it every day. This may be on your mirror, in your car, or on your calendar. Remember, you want to continually focus your subconscious mind on this image. You want to internalize it. This is your vision.

This vision will be the foundation for building your personal plan during the last section of this book. Included in the intervening chapters, you'll find many other concepts that you may want to incorporate in that plan. But through it all, keep your eye on how each concept contributes to the picture of your desired outcome.

"Two roads diverged in a wood and I—I took the one less
traveled by, and that has made all the difference."
—Robert Frost

CHAPTER 5

THE CIRCLE OF LIFE

An old proverb recommends an outline for the phases of life:

Ages 0-20:	Absorption. We learn.
Ages 20-40:	High-Energy Output. We produce and perform.
Ages 40-60:	Reflection. We evaluate our experiences.
Ages 60-80:	Mentoring. We pass the baton of knowledge.

I call the above process the circle of life because it starts with learning and ends with teaching. How appropriate it is for us to begin the journey of life by borrowing from those before us, and then to end our visit by giving back.

Sadly, the following is more typical of modern culture:

Ages 0-25:	Absorption. We learn.
Ages 25-65:	Scramble. We fight for all we can get.
Ages 65-80:	Check Out. We disappear from productive life.

What has happened? We have gone from intellectual learning to material earning—from giving to getting. While this has become a societal norm, it doesn't mean you have to live your life according to the second model. You can live on purpose. You are not a victim of society's fads. You are an activist in leading your own life.

And don't say, "I'm too old." That's an excuse for checking out. It's never too late to finish life well. Traditional thinking says that, as people get older, they resist change. Try reversing this: As people resist change, they start acting older!

IMPLEMENTATION TOOL: DEFINING YOUR CIRCLE

As you picture your future, ask yourself which circle of life best meets your desires.

Most people do not decide to alter their life's path. They keep doing whatever they have been doing until some outside force happens to them. This could be job loss, health problems, someone's death, war, etc.

Do you want this? Or do you want to proactively change your direction at different stages? Do you want life to happen to you, or do you want to happen to your life?

Frankly, either choice is acceptable. But "choice" is the key word.

> "Even if you are on the right track, you'll
> get run over if you just sit there."
> —Will Rogers

CHAPTER 6

MASTER YOUR DO LIST

We have a powerful enemy distracting us from our vision. I have personalized him by using the initials DL. He actually answers to several names including: Do List, To Be Dones, and Must Do's.

By whatever name, DL is especially dangerous because he comes disguised as a tool to help us get more done. The danger lies in the word "more." If we let him control our lives, he may succeed in helping us achieve more, but he will not necessarily teach us to prioritize. Our challenge is to turn the tables. If we become DL's master, we'll focus on the priority rather than the quantity of completed tasks.

Why not test ourselves by comparing the way we view money with the way we perceive time? If we are limited in the amount of money that we can spend (which most of us are), we conserve funds and make careful and calculated expenditures. Why not expend our time with the same attention to prioritizing? Time is far more important than money in the quest to reach our vision, yet we spend far more effort conserving money than we do conserving time.

This incongruity between the way we view money and the way we treat time results from the immediacy of the penalty for our respective mistakes. Misallocating our dollars results in a fairly quick consequence: We go broke. But squandering time may show no negative result until well into the future. Sadly, it's then too late. It is possible to recover financially, but misspent time is forever lost.

If we don't master DL, he'll gradually get us so focused on finishing every task that we'll forget our vision and just try to get through today. We'll come to think that a finished list equals a productive day. If our DL is getting longer each day, we feel we're failing. When we have fully bought into this logic, merely crossing items off the list becomes an end in itself. We ignore how pertinent these tasks actually are to our priorities.

Many of my clients have confessed to first doing the unimportant items on their to-do lists because there are more of them. This approach helps the list get shorter than if they do the (often tougher) priorities first. This is the ultimate result of DL's tyranny. In the end, he can rule our lives.

Stop. Think. Your to-do list will be full the day you die. But your vision may not be fulfilled. This happens because you can postpone long-term priorities without hearing them complain. But if you let him, DL will pester you every minute.

Okay, so if DL has so much destructive potential, why not just throw out the list and set ourselves free? I know people who have done this. They end up becoming DL's easiest victims. With no daily system, we increase our vulnerability to the most recent (or loudest) demand placed on us by others.

We need to control DL rather than destroy him. In fact, the more organized your daily system, the more you—not circumstances—control your expenditure of time.

IMPLEMENTATION TOOL: DESIGNING YOUR DO LIST

First, it may help you to stop calling it a "Do List." Switch to "Priority List" or "Action Notes." It's a small change that helps switch your focus from finished entries to priority items.

Next, picture each planned action as a mobile index card instead of a stationary entry on a list. Each item could contain the following ingredients:

- Title: It's what you call the action. So our index card reads "Clean Kitchen Cupboards" in the upper left corner.
- Date: It's when you want to be reminded again. Keep a fifty-two-week tabbed card file and pop the item into the week you desire.
- Priority: This is a good option if your list is huge. Put 1, 2, 3, etc. in the upper right corner to indicate priority.
- Daily Preview: During a morning card file review, pull the next three to six cards you plan to do.
- Action Notes: On the back of each card, keep your record of action, ideas for that project, names and phone numbers of people tied to that action, etc. These notes also help with monster projects, which are discussed in the next chapter.
- Electronic or Paper? If you're gadget-literate and willing to invest a few hundred dollars, an electronic organizer (PDA or pocket computer) makes the above system much easier.

"The wild things roared their terrible roars and gnashed their terrible teeth ... but Max stepped into his private boat and waved goodbye."
—Maurice Sendak, *Where the Wild Things Are*

CHAPTER 7

TAME THE MONSTERS

Some projects on your do list are so large or complex that they intimidate you. You don't even know where to start. So they just sort of take up permanent residence on your list—like an unwanted house guest. Examples of these monster tasks are:

- Seek a new job.
- Buy a new home.
- Find a new church.
- Clean the attic.
- Prepare income tax return.

My wife and I have a huge attic filled with twenty years' worth of junk. Our goal is to clean it. But this goal has taken up permanent residence on our list! It's just too large to think about. Actually, I think a fire may be the only solution. Fortunately, this goal is not critical to our vision.

Cleaning your attic might be a project that's important to your vision, in which case it will be a higher priority. Yet it seems so complex that you are mentally defeated every time you see it on your do list. As a result, you never do anything about it.

To conquer these intimidating projects, break them down into small steps. An item on your list that reads "order invitations" is far less intimidating than "plan the wedding." Similarly, "total up income records" is bite-sized compared to "prepare tax returns." And "organize the tool drawer" is far less discouraging than "clean the garage."

IMPLEMENTATION TOOL: TAMING THE MONSTERS

For practice, take one large project on your list and break it down into smaller steps. Keep the steps together as a note attached to the larger project. This way, you can see each item in the context of the whole.

As you complete small steps, you'll realize a major advantage of this system: Your sense of accomplishment will motivate you to progress even further toward finishing the whole project. Your initial sense of defeat will change to one of achievement.

"Our character is what we do when we think no one is looking."
—H. Jackson Brown, Jr.

CHAPTER 8

APPOINTMENTS WITH YOURSELF

Many years ago, I was driving to a dental appointment. I had spent a discouraging week chiding myself because I hadn't even touched my important projects. The last thing I needed was to sit in a dentist's chair. Right then, a thought struck me: I make time for appointments with others because they're on my calendar. Scheduling creates a mantle of urgency. So why not make appointments with myself for my priority projects?

This tool is a winner. At first blush, many people object to the idea because they say it will be too easy to postpone these appointments. True. But the key benefit is that it's on your calendar—in front of your face. If you decide to delay the appointment, immediately write it down for a new date and time.

A personal example might help. One of my life goals is to continually learn and expand my thinking. Therefore, a priority (and monster!) task is to periodically review my article file. Briefly explained, this is a file filled with material that I want to revisit because it interested me at the first read. The review time can always wait. But I don't want to postpone it indefinitely.

So I make a quarterly calendar entry noting, "Lunch: Article File." Do I postpone it? Almost always. Does it get done quarterly? Rarely. Does it get done more often than it otherwise would? Definitely!

You may choose to take your goal to coffee, to breakfast, to the park, for a walk, or on a picnic. I've seen clients effectively use all of the above locations.

But notice a common denominator: Take it away from the office. In this context, don't think of "office" in the traditional sense. Your office may be in a high-rise, in the kitchen, or anywhere else—it's the place where you are surrounded with reminders of all the other stuff you need to get done. Your traditional work location is where DL has the most influence. So get out of the "office" and turn off your pager, cell phone, and doorbell. For appointments with yourself, you need to get away to a place where your only focus is the project at hand.

IMPLEMENTATION TOOL: APPOINTMENTS WITH YOURSELF

Pick one of your monster tasks and set a time and date on your calendar to take it to a location away from your "office." When you finish this meeting with your project and before you leave, write the next date on your calendar.

Remember one rule: You cannot erase this appointment unless you reschedule it at that moment.

"Live the questions now. Perhaps then, someday far in the future, you will gradually, without even noticing it, live your way into the answer."
—Rainer Maria Rilke

CHAPTER 9

THE RIPENING OF A PROBLEM

Fruit needs to be ripe before you can fully enjoy it. Similarly, some problems need to ripen before they're ready to be solved. Trying to fix them when they're still in the green fruit stage creates a frustrating time trap. Let's begin by noting some problems that are commonly attacked when still under-ripe.

Although delegating problem-solving responsibilities can be a challenging task, allowing a problem broad ownership often leads to a faster solution. For example, if you are attempting to organize a group fundraiser but are having trouble coming up with innovative ideas, start by explaining the cause to a group of potential volunteers, and then give them time to absorb and internalize the concept. Be patient as you determine whether enough group energy and creativity builds around the idea. Once people sign on to the project, you will find that your preparation time not only speeds up implementation, but ensures a more involved and concerned group effort.

A second category of green fruit is almost an inversion of the first—a cause that you are interested in contributing to even though someone else is at the helm of problem-solving efforts. If your neighbor heatedly convinces you that a petition should be circulated in order to get an issue before the city council, his enthusiasm may prove contagious enough to pique your interest. Wait. If he needs your help and you believe in the issue at hand, you can provide your assistance when the time is right. But avoid dedicating yourself to every cause that catches your attention. By tomorrow evening, your neighbor may have prepared, circulated, and mailed the petition himself, and your energy can be saved for more pressing needs.

A third type of problem starts out green and then simply dies. Keep in mind that time or outside forces solve many issues, and you will likely save yourself a great deal of time and energy if you can employ patience in these situations. Imagine that your daughter comes home from the school playground complaining that Kevin pushed her off the slide and pulled her hair. You're tempted to call Kevin's parents. Instead, you wait. A week later, your daughter comes home happily exclaiming, "Kevin wrote me a love note today!"

Your daughter has learned a valuable life lesson without your interference—a lesson that shouldn't be discounted as a simple example of childhood behavior. Think of how often someone at work prematurely runs to the boss. In this type of situation, attentively allowing the problem to ripen often leads to a natural solution.

Finally, watch for green problems that stay green. They never become worthy of a solution. People tend to worry about everything that might happen in the future, yet many of these concerns never become reality. Even if they do, the challenge will be much better defined when the problem actually occurs. Say you're stewing about rumors that your employer might eliminate your job. You worry about the problem of unemployment. Later, the company does as expected, but you are moved to a different function. Now your challenge is developing new skills rather than finding a new job.

Of course, not all problems fit the green fruit description. As you learn to recognize those that do, you will save both energy and time. Learn to decipher between ripe and unripe problems by recognizing the symptoms discussed in this chapter.

When an apparent problem presents itself, take two simple steps. First, listen. After this, listen again. This second hearing gives you time to reflect. Notice how your doctor performs a diagnosis when you think you have a health problem. She listens. Then she asks more questions and listens again. Then she probes and examines. She does tests. She doesn't just rush into surgery.

Be willing to let today's problems mature a bit. Evaluate their urgency in light of the above diagnosis before you immediately give them your action or (worse) worry time.

IMPLEMENTATION TOOL:
EXAMINE FOR RIPENESS

Highlight any current priority-list item as "R" if you think the issue needs to ripen. Keep it on your list, but don't act on it immediately. Write down what ultimately happens. Save and review these notes periodically. You'll gain experience in recognizing green fruit.

> "Don't be afraid to take a big step. You can't
> cross a chasm in two small jumps."
> —David Lloyd George

CHAPTER 10

FORGET ABOUT JOBS

I spend some of my time with people who are looking for a job. In fact, one of my least favorite things to hear a person say is that he is looking for someone to give him a job—as if it were a donation.

Politicians talk about creating jobs. Individuals refer to getting a job. Parents brag about their child having a job. Human resources departments think about defining jobs. Middle-aged people are concerned with keeping their jobs. Yet many seniors look forward to the moment they can stop doing their jobs.

Hold it, folks. What are we doing here? Why do we focus on jobs? I thought we were going to hone in on goals.

To break this pattern, I introduce the following: Jobs are a very recent invention. Before the industrial revolution, people didn't have jobs. They had chores or tasks that they performed for the family farm or store. The goal was to sustain the operation. If your chore was done but your sister was sick, then you did your sister's tasks because you knew the goal.

To clarify this task-versus-goal viewpoint, let's look at an example: A person is in a job defined as billing service representative (BSR). His job is to handle billing problems from customers. One day, after he corrects an error, a caller tells him about a great idea for improving the product. The BSR responds with "Sorry, that's not my job." A potential opportunity is lost.

Now consider this alternate response from the BSR: "Tell me more about your idea so I can communicate it to the new product development department." If I were the employer or the customer, I would love this reaction. In this example, the BSR focused on the goal (the company's success)—just like on the farm one hundred years ago.

I often hear an objection to this suggestion for more goal-oriented action: "But I have a boss who would kill me if I did that. He'd say, 'Just do your job and shut up.'" If this sounds familiar, you need to do three things. First, finish this book so you have a personal plan and can gain focus and confidence in making a career change. Second, begin looking for an employer who wants employees to pursue the organization's goals. Third, get ready to help your associates find new occupations, because your current company is going to perform poorly.

There is one exception to this three-step recommendation. You may believe that your boss's attitude is not representative of the company as a whole and that top management would approve of your goal-oriented response to the customer. Without incriminating your direct boss, write a letter to a superior executive telling him or her about the idea and requesting a transfer into a more communicative department. "But I'll be fired," you exclaim. My friend, if that happens, you have just been denied a seat on an airplane that's going to crash.

But don't be so sure it will happen. On a daily basis, I work with executives in top management positions, and I can testify to their desperate search for people who will focus on goals instead of currently defined procedures (otherwise known as jobs). Your top management is likely concerned that middle managers are not nurturing input from the people who are in direct contact with the customer. Here's a well-kept secret: Most executive-level managers know that you're scared to talk to them about the real stuff that's going on—and they hate this fact! They're constantly searching for ways to get in touch with what's really happening in their corporation.

Here's a recent story that exemplifies this entire process. I was shopping at X Store, which is a major international chain. Their headquarters are located in a temperate climate, but I was in their store in northern Michigan in April, where it was still about forty degrees. I asked the store manager, "Where are your fire logs?" She answered, "Incredibly, we had to ship them all back to the supplier in March." You can picture my management-coaching brain responding to her word "incredibly." So I had some fun. I asked, "Why do you say 'incredibly'?" She rolled her eyes and complained, "We can sell fire logs until Memorial Day in northern Michigan, but headquarters won't listen to us because they live where it's warm by now."

It probably won't surprise you that my next question was, "Why don't you call the president?" She laughed and quipped, "My boss would kill me." I pursued further with, "Why? Doesn't your boss want more sales?" Her response came thoughtfully. "Well, he does, but he doesn't want to fight with headquarters."

Before we diagnose this conversation, it might help you to know that the president of this company is experiencing a languishing stock price, declining investor confidence, and a competitor who is beating his company every quarter. He inherited his position from a founder who was world-renowned for customer focus. What's happening here?

What's happening is that the store manager, her regional boss, and the clerk at HQ are all focusing on their jobs—not on the goal. If the store manager called or wrote to the president, he would be horrified—and not only about fire logs in northern Michigan.

He would think, "If the system isn't working there, how many millions is it costing me elsewhere?"

He'd wonder, "Why am I not getting this kind of input from other places? How have I shut down communication?"

He would ask himself, "What's wrong with my management process? How do I get my staff to open up the communication process to get store managers' input into the decision-making process? How do we get the HQ group to sense and feel the customer breathing down their necks?"

In short, this input to the president will confirm all his worst fears about how distant he has become from the customer. More important, the store manager will know that she focused on the goal rather than just thinking about her job. Long term, her focus on this habit will help her direct employees to the goal—to what really matters.

IMPLEMENTATION TOOL: REDEFINING YOUR JOB

Write down a re-definition of your current job in terms of what the goals are. If you were the owner of the company you now work for, how would you define what you do in terms of results to be accomplished, not just tasks to be performed? In addition to the job definition your employer gave you, define your performance criteria in terms of these goals.

"Criticism has the power to do good when there is something
to be destroyed, dissolved, or reduced. But it is capable
only of harm when there is something to be built."
—Dr. Carl Jung

CHAPTER 11

FIND YOUR POWER ALLEY

A few years ago, I heard an interesting anecdote on the radio that led me to this example: Imagine that I decide to form a new organization called Animal University, and I ask you to invest your money and time in this effort. Here's my pitch for this new educational venture:

We're going to teach students to improve their performance. We're going to focus on four target markets: rabbits, eagles, ducks, and squirrels. We will teach the rabbits to fly better. We'll train the eagles to jump higher. Our focus for the ducks will be better climbing, and we'll train the squirrels to swim.

I hope you would choose to invest your time and money elsewhere. Eagles don't jump well, but they are glorious flyers. I've never seen a duck climb a tree, but they sure know how to swim. You get the picture.

If you think my Animal University focus is so misguided, then why is this exactly how we treat people in our schools, organizations, and (very sadly) families? We seem more comfortable looking at our weaknesses than our strengths. Let's explore why this is.

Trace this story and see if it resonates with you. You have some natural strengths, attributes, and talents. You've probably had these since you were in your teens. You're accustomed to them; they're natural and instinctive. So, for example, let's say I tell you, "You're really good at relating." Essentially, I'm telling you that you're gifted in the area of empathy—at climbing into someone else's shoes. You're probably a great listener and care about others' feelings. You tend to see their uniqueness and respect it, relating to people because you naturally care about them—not because you can get something from them.

What's your response to this input from me? You might say (even if only to yourself), "Yeah, so what? Isn't everyone that way?" You consider this attribute a given, a natural, an instinct. You've lived with it for so long that it's no big deal to you.

However, my answer to you is, "No, everyone is not empathetic." You're surprised. You've gotten so accustomed to this attribute that you don't recognize it as a major strength.

Now, if I turn the tables and start discussing your weaknesses, you will become much more comfortable. This is because you're familiar with this discussion. For years, you've heard about your weaknesses. Your teachers, managers, parents, and others have talked about these. You're accustomed to focusing on your deficiencies.

Let's test ourselves with a parenting question. You can either consider your own children (if you have any) or think about the way your parents would have reacted in this situation. A child comes home from school with the results of two final exams. She received an A in English. She also received an F in math. How do the parents react? Which grade gets discussed first?

I hope your answer was the English grade. But I fear many of us know instinctively that the math grade would have been the first topic, and not because we believe that math is more important. If that's your argument, reverse the grades. For most of us, the failure seems more pressing an issue than the success.

The fact is, we don't succeed by fixing weaknesses. We succeed by optimizing our strengths. Yet, ironically, we spend most of our time focusing on our deficiencies. Let's stop this and reverse the process. Let's work on optimizing our power alleys.

Here is a list of attributes that will help you evaluate yourself. My experience is that you should expect to find one to three of these as your primary strengths.

- Communicator: Is good at writing and speaking to others, getting a point across, and inspiring.

- Conceptualizer: Sees patterns, strategies, and alternatives; has purpose; plans and envisions the big picture.
- Creator: Acts on new ideas; is inspired to make change happen and acts quickly to create it; is impatient, risk tolerant, and spontaneous.
- Decider: Has a confident and self-assured presence; directs decisions and often dominates; is more likely to say, "Let's try it."
- Developer: Serves as a mentor, teacher, and encourager; appreciates teamwork and delegates well; is often self-effacing and focused on others' goals, working behind the curtain to help others achieve.
- Driver: Measures and keeps score; is a self-starter who likes to win and will often raise the bar.
- Learner: Is focused on continuous learning; recalls history; seeks to know and understand more than to take action.
- Logician: Is introspective, analytical, and often serious; looks for causes, effects, and logical flows of events.
- Organizer: Appreciates structure, organization, and routine; is consistently detailed, precise, and focused; excels at follow-up and arranging outcomes.
- Persuader: Commands others, often relating in order to achieve a certain end result; frequently wins others to his or her view.
- Power Player: Seeks personal recognition or fame in order to enhance his or her own control; appreciates feeling significant; is able to manipulate situations and control others.
- Reconciler: Solves conflicts among others, helping a team move forward together; works to develop a consensus.
- Relater: Is empathetic and cares about others' feelings; listens and relates to others naturally, without trying to achieve a certain result; sees people's uniqueness and seeks out those who are often ignored.
- Fulfiller: Feels obligation and takes the necessary load; follows through on promises.

IMPLEMENTATION TOOL: ATTRIBUTES ANALYSIS

Let's focus on your natural talents. Since you've likely been beaten up over your weaknesses for a long time, this may be a tough project. Your gifted areas probably aren't at the top of your mind.

To make it easier, try enlisting the help of people who have known you since you were at least fifteen. These people may include siblings, long-time friends, teachers, or parents. When you ask them about your strengths, you'll be surprised how often they answer, "You're kidding, right?" It's obvious to them; they see your natural talents, but you don't. You're too accustomed to these attributes.

But listen to these long-time associates. They can see much in you that you may not see in yourself.

"A diamond with a flaw is more valuable than a brick without a flaw."
—William J.H. Boetcker

CHAPTER 12

WHAT ABOUT WEAKNESSES?

So, if it's so important to focus on your power alleys, then what do you do about weaknesses? Do we now just ignore our deficiencies?

Before we decide what (if anything) to do about our shortcomings, let's look at how strengths and weaknesses work in our lives.

Many of us have been taught that we're talented in certain areas and deficient in others. But instead of this black-and-white paradigm, think about strengths and weaknesses on a continuum. In other words, rather than envisioning your intellect as a light switch that can be turned from on to off, picture a dimmer switch that turns the light down gradually. This dimmer moves from left to right:

Natural—Available—Unavailable

On the far left is your strength (or strengths)—the skill that comes naturally to you. It's like breathing. Actually, you can't *not* do it. For example, if you have a tendency toward the trait of empathy, you don't *decide* to see people's feelings or climb into their shoes—you just do it. You can't help it.

On the other hand, if your level of empathy is in the middle of the continuum, you only have this attribute available to you if you focus on it. But you have to think about it or plan ahead in order to practice it. You go into a room, talk to a person, and *if* you plan in advance to concentrate on his or her problem, you can be empathetic.

Available attributes are analogous to a tool you own and keep in your garage but don't carry with you all day on your tool belt. If you're dealing with a weakness in this middle land of available, you can practice it, get coaching to build it up, and study ways to strengthen it in your arsenal of tools. But a word of caution: Try not to set your sights on making it a natural strength. You may discourage yourself (unless the trait is already very close to the left side of your continuum).

To further the example, if you're at the right end of the continuum, you don't have empathy available to you. Even if you want to, you can't practice it. It just doesn't work for you. For your unavailable traits, I frankly suggest you choose from three options: balance it, soften it, or ignore it.

Let's start with balancing. This is the process of deliberately spending time with people who have opposite natural attributes to your own. Let's say I'm a natural relater, but logic is unavailable to me. You are a natural logician, but relational skills are unavailable to you. We go to a party together.

When I walk into the room, I gravitate toward the people who appear to be hurting or unhappy, and consider how I can connect with them. I don't even have to think about this. It's as natural as breathing.

Meanwhile, you connect with the serious discussions in the room. You overhear a couple of my conversations and think they don't make sense. At the end of the evening, I would likely say, "She was hurting so badly." You'd be likely to respond, "So why doesn't she just do something to fix it?"

The point is, we're both correct. But no matter how hard I try, I cannot conjure up the logical analysis that you find so naturally. And no matter how much you focus, you cannot create an awareness of emotional issues.

But there's also a middle ground between these extremes. I can learn from our differences—and so can you. In fact, that's how we grow.

I don't have to fix my weakness; I just have to see who excels where I am less strong, and then learn to count on that person in challenging situations. This is the balancing process.

Here's how our story plays out. Over time, I watch you use your logician approach, and you watch me use my relational approach. If we have teachable hearts, as we watch and learn, we begin to see the strength in each other's attributes.

Note that this doesn't mean I eliminate my so-called weakness, nor do you omit yours. But we each begin to act as a sort of sandpaper on each other's rough edges.

Make no mistake about how tough this is. You're going to have to move to a mindset that accepts—and actually admires—those with attributes opposite from your own. You're going to actually seek these people out, not just put up with them. You will come to recognize them as the balancers in your life.

The tough thing about this is that we often gravitate toward like-minded people and avoid those who are opposite. But in order to benefit from the balancing concept, we must spend time with people who seem most different.

The next option you have in dealing with a weakness is to soften it. This is easier than balancing. In softening, you learn some parts of practicing this attribute. Begin by admitting to yourself that you are probably not going to make this trait a strength. You're just going to learn some aspects of the talent. In effect, you're going to be an amateur practitioner.

To continue our contrast of logical and relational traits, your softening process might involve you proactively thinking about each person at the party before you arrive. You might focus on tuning your thoughts to their feelings instead of to what you know to be your natural propensity toward logical issues. At the beginning, many of your actions may seem strange, like you're acting a part in a play. Actually, in a sense, you are. But give it time. Practicing a behavior can eventually change your attitude, which in turn makes the behavior more genuine.

The last option with a weakness is to ignore it. This one shocks a lot of listeners. Not everything can be fixed, nor should it be. It may simply not be worth it. Remember that optimizing your power alleys is going to be the way to success. If balancing a key deficiency doesn't work and softening its edges doesn't succeed, then I'd suggest you ignore it. And one of the best tools to use for this is humor.

Don't be afraid to say out loud, "I'm not good at relational stuff. I've tried. It's not going to happen. I'm a person with a strong logician trait. But, hey, you can call on me to fix your computer problem, and I'll try to chat over coffee while I'm there." Who knows? You might become a little better at relational attributes while you get called on in your strength area.

IMPLEMENTATION TOOL: MANAGING WEAKNESSES

List your weaknesses under three headings: balance, soften, or ignore. For those that fit under balance, think about a partner who is opposite from you and spend time with that person. For the weaknesses that you'd like to soften, find a coach/helper to prepare you for the occasions when you'll be exposed to this deficiency. For the ignore category, set yourself free! Admit this weakness out loud; you may help others do the same.

"Live as if you were to die tomorrow.
Learn as if you were to live forever."
—Mahatma Gandhi

CHAPTER 13

EDUCATION

Many of us have made a critical mistake. We have come to value education in terms of what job it helps us obtain. Watch for this erroneous education/job connection the next time you're with a mixed group of students and middle-aged adults. Listen to the older person's questions to the younger. "What are you studying to be?" and "What can you do with that major?" are often primary inquiries.

When we view learning primarily as a career ticket, we dilute its potential contribution to our own life purpose and risk giving poor advice to our children and others.

You may wonder how one is expected to earn a living while adhering to this theory. Don't get the wrong impression. I'm not saying that people don't need to work, accomplish, or create in order to achieve goals. My point is that an older person advising today's youth about job-based education is on shaky ground; today's job market is a different world.

The older you are, the more likely it is that you grew up when education meant learning a job-related skill. And that skill may have served you well for an entire career. In contrast, today's student has read statistics predicting that 40 percent of the occupations that will be available in ten years do not even exist today. So the purpose of modern education should not be mastery of specific job skills, but development of critical thinking and, even more important, a love of continuous learning.

Kathy goes to school in 1920 to study typing so she can get a job transcribing. She is excellent at her work and has a fair amount of job security. Toward the end of her career in 1960, she is using improved equipment but still employs the same skills she learned in school. That same year, John (her grandson) enters school to study the same job-oriented skill. In the year 2000 he's using computer equipment but still employing his keyboard training. Unfortunately, John's daughter Susie accepts his advice and sets the same job-oriented goal for her education. Before Susie even graduates, nobody types anymore! She can't find a job because a new technology is developed to transcribe voice directly to print.

Well-intentioned and loving advice from parents and grandparents doesn't change the fact that Susie is ill-prepared for her world. She is well-prepared for Kathy's 1920s world.

Okay, so how do we deal with planning education when today's rapidly accelerating pace of change has begun severing the direct link between jobs and schooling? A simple perspective change might be helpful: Rather than thinking of learning as a means of obtaining a job, take your general knowledge and continuing education into consideration.

When planning your schooling, include as many general knowledge courses as you can. Even if you are specializing or taking a vocational approach, don't ignore the importance of these subjects. If you don't think you can carry the workload, audit them. The following skills and mental disciplines are both enduring and exceedingly valuable, not only in regards to career-related endeavors, but for all life skills:

- Love of learning
- Reading comprehension and speed
- Relating to others
- Teamwork
- Verbal and written communication
- Creativity
- Critical thinking
- Quantitative comprehension
- Historical perspective
- Logic
- Foreign language
- Appreciation of the arts

Next—and please think of this as a change in stride more than your next step—plan to continue your education throughout your life. Look at the first item in the above list. Forget about the old system where you learned a skill, practiced it, and then retired. Fill each day with learning. Read, listen, watch, ask questions, explore, travel, think, take courses, seek out training sessions, etc. Open your mind to using some savings to quit your job and go back to school. Don't be afraid of this last one. Money is better placed in your head than in your toys.

IMPLEMENTATION TOOL: EDUCATION

Set at least one goal, with due date, focused on learning something new.

Every time you see a word or concept you don't know, look it up immediately, write down the definition, and add it to your priority list with a one-month follow-up. If you don't know it in a month, forward it to a future date until you do.

Whenever you hear (or ask) a question and don't know the answer, look it up and put it on your list until you've got it cold.

Sign up for one course of study on a subject you'd like to know more about. Go with your passion on this—perhaps cooking, photography, or mathematics. For other ideas, use this chapter's list of skills and mental disciplines.

"In the business world, everyone is paid in two coins: cash and experience. Take the experience first; the cash will come later."
—Harold S. Geneen

CHAPTER 14

FINANCIAL COMPENSATION

A large number of my clients finish their personal planning process with income very high on their goal lists. Because of this, they tend to take a lot of exit ramps from their long-term plans in response to short-term opportunities to make more money. Instead of taking this route, consider focusing on your value rather than on the amount of money you can accumulate. In the end, you'll be more likely to succeed in every respect because, quite simply, people are willing to pay more for something valuable.

How can you increase your value? Memorize the QDS formula. Value is determined by the Quality of, Demand for, and Scarcity of your capabilities. It's easy to see how these three factors determine what an employer or customer pays you. Simply turn the tables and consider how you decide to spend your own money.

Let's say you're car shopping and I am the auto dealer. I want to sell you a used compact model with a small engine by promoting its good gas mileage. Your needs, however, do not meet this description. You need seats for eight and a large towing capacity. Since your personal needs and desires determine quality, this small car won't score very high in the Q category. In addition, you've read articles that tell you that the car I am trying to sell is unpopular with the public (low D), which could be why you count twenty-five duplicate models in my lot and make your own judgment on S.

It looks like I will either lose the sale or, at best, lose some money in order to meet the price you are willing to pay.

In this example, do you care how much money I need you to pay me so I can meet my goals? Are you concerned about what it cost to manufacture the car? No! You make your decision based on your evaluation of QDS. An employer or client utilizes the same formula to determine your value.

Audiences have presented me with three apparent exceptions to the QDS equation: luck, restrictive employment contracts, and government subsidy. It's true that each of these can violate our formula. But before you bet your future on them, let's review the risks of each one.

First, what about luck (and her cousin, timing)? Sure, you might inherit a fortune or win the lottery. But since you can't count on luck, it doesn't belong in your planning process. And don't miss the subtlety that luck is sometimes a poor man's explanation for a rich man's hard work.

The second exception to QDS can appear when your income is protected by a restrictive employment contract. For example, some union agreements set pay based on same-pay-for-same-job, seniority, and other non-QDS criteria. In this environment, you may possess great skill (high Q) and get paid the same as a low-Q colleague. Yes, such contracts escape the logic of QDS, and they may restrict your income potential. So if financial success is high on your goal list, consider building your value and changing jobs.

Third, some people feel immune to the QDS formula because they are protected by government subsidy. Laws can be passed to fix prices, limit competition, or create artificial demand through government purchases. Like unionization, this can interrupt the QDS link between value and income. But be warned: If such methods support your income, take small comfort in this apparent escape hatch. If your industry loses political clout or the government becomes fickle, politicians can take away what they have given.

In summary, you may escape QDS in the short run through one of the above exceptions. If you're close enough to retirement, your financial compensation may even stay protected until you stop working. But be cautious about recommending the same route to your children; luck, contracts, and laws can change, but the QDS formula will stay in force.

Finally, here is a challenging question to think about when determining your own QDS value: If you took the risk of starting your own company and put all your personal savings at stake, would you hire you? Why, or why not?

IMPLEMENTATION TOOL: SELF-VALUATION

Do you want your income to increase next year? List your plans for increasing your value. When you look at this list, does it justify an increase in income?

If you are now artificially protected from the value formula via a non-sustainable contract or subsidy, use your spare time to re-train yourself (as discussed in our Education chapter) so your value can stand on its own.

Evaluate your answer to the last question about hiring yourself. If you didn't answer the question, why not?

"The indispensable first step to getting the
things you want out of life is this:
decide what you want."
—Ben Stein

CHAPTER 15

WHAT DO YOU
WANT TO DO?

A huge number of people are struggling with what they want to do. In this context, "do" usually refers to a career decision. But people also seek help in deciding how they want to spend their volunteer time or what they want to do in retirement.

Young people nearing the end of their formal education tell me, "Everyone asks me the same question, but the fact is, I just don't know what I want to do." Parents of these young adults lament, "She's really a great kid, but she doesn't know what she wants to do." Clients in their twenties who are involved in their first jobs often observe, "I'm not sure that this is what I want to do for the rest of my life." Middle-career people wonder aloud, "Am I really doing what I want to do?" Close to the end of their careers, clients say, "I've thought about retiring, but I don't know what I'll do."

It is a sad fact that a huge number of us simply keep doing what we're doing because of inertia—the law of physics stating that a body at rest will stay at rest until acted on by an outside force. In short, a soccer ball sits still until kicked. Similarly, we tend to keep doing what we're doing until outside circumstances force change upon us. But living intentionally requires that we lead our own lives rather than wait for external forces to kick us into motion.

It's true that change requires energy and risk, but inertia can be even riskier. You could end up like so many people who come to dread what they do. When they wake up in the morning, they look ahead and can't wait until quitting time, vacation, or the weekend.

Or you could become the person who wakes up and can't wait to get into his day. It is an incredible blessing to experience this mindset. You'll see positive changes in how you feel about yourself, treat your family, and react to others.

Whether you are an individual in the work force, a stay-at-home parent, a volunteer, or a retiree, it's likely that you don't fall into either one of the above categories. You may not be seriously unhappy with what you do, but you are not truly positive about it either. If you fall into this group, you probably wonder if you're really doing what you want to do.

Whichever description fits—dread, love, or questioning—the exercise below will help you find answers to job-related confusions. It works because it's based on a fact that surprises many: Subconsciously, you know more about what you want to do than you may realize.

IMPLEMENTATION TOOL: FINDING WHAT YOU WANT

Start a Love and Dread List. In the following two exercises, you are going to uncover the things that really light your fire and those that dampen the flames.

As you start your day and think through upcoming events, list the items you really look forward to. Also list items that you want to delay or avoid altogether. Keep this list going for several weeks.

As you go back through your life (all the way to childhood), what are the things you have consistently looked forward to and the things you have tried to avoid? Ask old friends and family members for their insight on this.

Don't try to finish the above list in one sitting. Keep your notes for a couple of months. Most likely, you'll make additions over time.

As you see your real passions emerge from this analysis, ask yourself three questions: In what you now do, what passions are not utilized? Can you expand your current primary occupation to include these missing elements? If not, what new pursuits make better use of your passions?

Study the above list and look for patterns. This is a critical step because you don't want to give too much weight to an isolated love or dread event. You will benefit most from concentrating on frequently occurring patterns.

Searching for patterns in your love and dread list may seem difficult at first. Some of the following examples and ideas will help.

Let's say your dread list includes a phone call you must make to Rick about a billing problem. Standing alone, this single item tells us little. It could mean that you don't like dealing with Rick, in which case it's a pretty localized negative. Or, dreading this call might be a broader indicator of your aversion to accounting or quantitative details. Going even deeper, it may reveal that you avoid conflict. You must find a repeat pattern before the true meaning will become clear.

"I don't want to give my speech tonight to the Junior League." This is simply an isolated event if it has to do with not being prepared or not feeling well that day. If you find it's a pattern, you could have the (very common) fear of public speaking.

"I feel down about giving Leslie her negative performance review at lunch today." This may just be related to Leslie and how she reacts to things. But if this type of dread is a trend, you may have a tendency to choose your own popularity over your organization's performance.

As you review your conclusions from this exercise, keep in mind that you may be able to change what you dread. You don't have to simply live with it. One client dreaded public speaking but loved the other components of her vocation. So she decided to re-train herself to appreciate the positives of speaking in front of others. This is laudable. If you love most of what you do, try fixing the parts you dislike.

Finally, if you can't fix the negatives of your current endeavor, there is a less scary remedy than changing careers. However, it's only recommended if your occupation contains mostly "loves" limited by one "dread" category. In this case, try substitution therapy—minimizing the effect of the dislike by focusing maximum time on the activities you do like.

Say your pattern shows that you love the individual achievement you had in your old job as a commissioned salesman. Now you've been promoted to a job requiring team performance. The job's great except for the teamwork part. In this case, practicing substitution therapy could mean taking up individualized hobbies (like marathon racing or piano lessons) to satisfy your passion for solo performance.

You could use this same substitution idea if you love relating to people but you work alone. Try focusing your free time on group activities like visiting nursing home residents or joining an athletic league.

If none of the solutions works, at least your homework will give you confidence in the fact that you now know what you really want to do. That's a big step in deciding to change. And change is what most people dread.

"I once knew a man who grabbed a cat by the tail.
He learned 40% more about cats than the man who didn't."
—Mark Twain

CHAPTER 16

FAIL FAST AND FORWARD

Picture yourself visiting me at my lakeside home in winter. It's ten degrees below zero and the lake is covered with ice. You ask me, "Can I safely walk across the lake?" I answer you by explaining that the lake is two miles across, it has been below freezing for seven weeks, and there's a river entering your path whose current tends to undermine the ice and make its depth unpredictable.

Have I answered your question? No. Welcome to life. You confront an important decision with some information, but not with everything you need to be completely satisfied and sure of your choice.

So would you walk across the ice? Before you read on, make your decision.

Now let's add a piece of input. I tell you that the lake is two feet deep all the way across. That made your decision a bit easier, didn't it? Your risk of failure has decreased dramatically. Notice that you have no more information about the thickness of the ice; instead, you have increased information about the cost of failure. Now your decision is more about your willingness to get wet than your willingness to drown. That's a very different choice!

If you walk across thin ice, fall in, get wet, and don't drown, then I suggest you failed fast and forward; you made a decision and then you learned. Many of us are so concerned with avoiding failure (falling through the ice) that we actually focus too little on success (getting across the lake). The fact is, the right decision is most often unknowable. So instead of waiting for all the answers, consider moving forward more quickly and learning from your decision. In other words, fail fast and forward.

Note that when I encourage you to fail fast, I'm not inviting you to fail or suggesting that failure is good. Rather, I'm asking you to make decisions with less information than you'd ideally like to have. I'm suggesting that you'll have a better chance at success if you take risks, act, and move forward rather than sit still.

Think of pushing a parked car. When it's sitting still, it's virtually impossible to move. Now, start the ignition and put it in motion—even if you're going in the wrong direction. Once you've gotten it moving, it will be much easier to push it where you want it to go.

Get yourself moving; don't worry so much about direction. You can fix that once you get some momentum.

Inevitably, life is filled with choices for which you have 20 to 60 percent of the information you'd like to have. For many of us, this lack of data creates trepidation, which leads to paralysis, i.e., "I don't know enough to move forward." Well, you probably never will know as much as you'd like. And if, eventually, you have the facts you need to ease your misgivings, by the time you've gathered the information, it will probably be too late for your decision to have any impact.

Let's look at this first fail-fast step in a little more detail. Imagine that you have a choice to make and you're getting input from people on the options you have available. After several inputs, you start hearing repeats, redundant arguments, and feedback that is adding little further light to your path. This doesn't mean you have all the facts you want. But it may mean you have received 80 percent of the information you're going to get.

At this point, consider that if you don't make a decision, you have no chance of making the right decision. So, at the 80/20 point, just go for it!

Now let's look at the second half of this system I'm offering you—the fail forward part. This refers to learning from what you did with your imperfect knowledge rather than dwelling on your failure.

Many of us think we have a lot of experience. But "a lot" is a relative term. Think about this: Do you have a wide range of experience? Or have you repeated the same incident again and again?

In other words, have you really learned from events in your life? Have you studied them? Have you written them in your journal and reviewed them? Have you revisited them in your mind and chewed on the lessons to be learned? What's challenging here is remembering to review a decision and keep track of the lessons. But take the time to do it; these steps are critical in failing forward.

It's exhilarating to me to review the so-called failures of some very successful people. Perhaps that sounds cynical, but in fact, it's just the opposite. Rather, I admire their ability to learn from their mistakes and move on. I keep the following list with me for inspiration in the foggiest moments of uncertainty:

- Isaac Newton did poorly in grade school and was listed as unpromising.
- When Einstein presented his PhD dissertation, the University of Bern rejected it. They called it irrelevant and fanciful.
- Michael Jordan was cut from his high-school basketball team.
- A newspaper editor fired Walt Disney because he supposedly lacked imagination and had no good ideas.
- Winston Churchill failed the sixth grade.
- Babe Ruth struck out 1,300 times. A major league record.
- Dr. Seuss's first children's book was rejected by twenty-three publishers.

The issue is not failing. The issue is failing to learn.

IMPLEMENTATION TOOL: JOURNAL

As you face a decision, write down your thoughts, the input you're getting from others, and the tensions you're facing in making the choice. After you make the decision, journal the outcomes. Make a follow-up note to review these notes one year later. As you look up your past notes, learn from what you faced. Did you need all the facts? Were your fears exaggerated? What did you learn from the decision?

"The true meaning of life is to plant trees, under
whose shade you do not expect to sit."
—Nelson Henderson

CHAPTER **17**

GIVING

We're all surrounded by messages that motivate us to give our money and/or time. Philanthropic organizations recite their needs and the needs of the people or causes they serve. While it is true that these organizations need money, I submit to you that the reverse is also true. It is we who need to give.

This need comes from inside you. It is representative of your built-in requirement for human contact, love, and a sense of accomplishment. A shortage of giving will leave you unfulfilled in life.

This includes sharing your money and time, but even that's too limited. Giving encompasses contributing your genuine caring, wisdom, and experience to others. Often, the most a person requires is the donation of an open ear or a bit of honest insight.

Giving focuses you away from yourself. Consider J.A. Holmes's astute observation: "It is well to remember that the entire population of the universe, with one trifling exception, is composed of others." You and I are a very tiny part of what's going on in the world. If we continually concentrate on ourselves, we eventually will achieve total aloneness. Oh sure, you may find yourself with lots of "friends" if you focus on building your own material wealth. But how many would be by your side if you ran into financial trouble?

We are designed to be a part of something larger than ourselves. If we ignore the fact that this is engineered into us, we are like a man who knows his car was intended to drive on land but nonetheless decides to steer it into the river. He may float for a period of time, but inevitably he will sink.

Giving exposes you to new wisdom for your own life. When you give your time, energy, mentoring, or ear to others, you learn. You see things from a new perspective. You gain insight. When you donate your money, its grip on your life is weakened. The more you send forth, the more clarity you bring to your own life.

Many people become enthusiastically unselfish with their money and time only after something negative happens to their comfortable lives; suddenly they find themselves among the needy for the first time. After getting help from others, these folks become major proponents of giving. Maybe you can picture feeling this way, but you can't remember ever being on the receiving end. Here's news for you: You have been!

You may not have recognized this because it's easy to take many gifts for granted. Perhaps you were blessed with no physical impairments. Maybe you're free of mental illness. You could have a high level of natural intelligence or, at least, a lack of learning disabilities. You might live in a country in which freedom allows you to pursue your talents. How many gave their lives to give you that gift? Did a past teacher, parent, or friend give you encouragement or guidance?

As you see the reality of what you've received, how do you feel about what you give?

IMPLEMENTATION TOOL: GIVING

Pick just one person to whom you are going to give without any expectation of return. Make this first choice up-close and personal. In other words, don't just write a check to an organization.

Write down how you feel about giving before you try it. Then read these comments back to yourself after the experiment.

"An honest answer is a sign of true friendship."
—Proverbs 24:26

CHAPTER 18

ACCOUNTABILITY PARTNERING

When you tell your boss your job goals, she is going to check back and see how you're doing. If you commit to an exercise plan with your personal trainer, he will ask how you did last week. After telling the committee chairperson you will have the invitations mailed on the fifteenth of the month, the leader will check on your deadline. We even let children hold us responsible for our plans ("But, Daddy, you promised we could go to the zoo today").

This is accountability. We are all accustomed to it. This idea of being held responsible reminds us that we have made a promise to someone. We have set an objective, and we expect the other party to remind us of our commitment.

Since the above examples are so acceptable to us, why do we avoid the same accountability when it comes to achieving our visions? Why don't we have an outside influence holding us responsible for our personal plans? Think about establishing your own "boss" for these goals. Let's call this person (or people) our accountability partner(s).

I used to tell myself, "I really want to quit smoking." But I didn't want anyone checking with me on a regular basis, asking, "So, Bill, how ya doin' with the smoking?" I wanted to believe that I was gaining on my goal. Outside input might have shattered that illusion.

Once I finally invited other people to hold me accountable, I actually did quit smoking. And my partners were a major factor in my success.

Make sure to go beyond verbal commitment. Give your partner a list of your goals. You may meet with her and explain that you are on the right track, but when she shows you your own writing, it might become clear that you are nowhere close to your plan. This technique ensures that she won't have to challenge your performance evaluation—your own words will be right there in front of you.

An example may be helpful. When my father was in his fifties, he would often comment, "Son, if you see me behaving like [this or that] when I'm older, please tell me. I don't want to do that." Twenty years later, when he was acting that way, I did as requested. Repeatedly, he would become angry with me and reject the input. So I eventually stopped telling him.

To avoid this, my wife and I have asked our three daughters to be our accountability partners regarding our own old-age goals. We have given them the letter below so they can simply show it to us when we're off track. When they call us to task, we'll see our own words and signatures, so we can't blame them for the input. The latest update:

June 2, 2005

Dearest Daughters:
We would like you to be our accountability partners. We want to be intentional about the way we grow old. We want to finish well.
Please call our attention to how we're doing with the list below. We expect to add to it over time as we think of new items. If so, we'll keep you covered!
   Love, Mom and Dad

Mom and Dad's Mission
Statement About Growing Old
- *Don't do the same thing every day at the same time.*
- *Stay involved with young people.*
- *Give ourselves away every day.*
- *We do not want to do nothing; we want to be contributing to something worthwhile.*
- *Keep our family-oriented vision in mind. E.g., We planned on a grocery store trip this afternoon. Then we get a surprise opportunity to take a boat trip with the family. Let's not choose the grocery store!*

As with any examples I give, please don't assume that our goals have to be yours. I just want to show you the value of the written goals that you reveal to your accountability partner.

One last suggestion on this subject: When you try your first accountability meeting, don't give your partner your entire life plan and all your goals. Start with one key objective, even if it's a small one. You both need to get comfortable with this process before you proceed. You also want to test your chosen person to be certain you're both at ease with her role as it relates to the specific goal you are discussing. In addition, you may want to choose different partners for different objectives.

IMPLEMENTATION TOOL: ACCOUNTABILITY PARTNERS

Your choice of accountability partners should be determined by the following factors:

- You trust them.
- You care what they think.
- They care about you personally.
- You can admit failure to them.

You may choose one or several people for any of your goals depending on how much perspective that specific objective requires.

Meet with your partner(s) to explain accountability. Beforehand, a copy of this chapter or book may be a helpful gift to give your partner.

Give your accountability partner a written copy of the items for which you want to be held responsible. Then set a follow-up date. Set an appointment on your calendars for that time. This date will force you to evaluate your performance because you know the review is coming.

As discussed above, partners are often a big help. But you may prefer to do it alone. This can be especially true when you're new to the process. So let's turn to the subject of using yourself as your accountability partner.

"You cannot teach a man anything; you can
only help him find it within himself."
—Galileo

CHAPTER 19

PARTNERING WITH YOURSELF

The problem I have had with holding myself responsible is my tendency to rewrite history. I look at a goal and say, "Yeah, I'm doing okay with that one." Or I say, "Well, I must not have meant to state that goal in that way." In short, I bend the goal to match the results.

Try a simple exercise to solve this problem. Remember the letter to your partner in the prior chapter? This is similar. I call it tapping myself on the shoulder. It's a reminder of what I wanted to do.

IMPLEMENTATION TOOL:
SELF-PARTNERING

Write yourself a letter. Put a note in your calendar to review it at a future date. Alternatively, give it to a friend in a self-addressed envelope and ask him to mail it to you later. Seeing your own goal written in your own words is immensely powerful. You can't ignore it.

Here's a great idea made possible by today's technology: You can write yourself an e-mail and postdate it for the day you want the reminder sent. What could be simpler?

Once you have read your letter, amend or expand your goals as appropriate and give it back to your friend to send again so that you can continuously track your progress. Think about this idea in terms of your experiences in the workplace. You get notes from your boss about your performance as compared to company goals. Similarly, if you want to be the boss of your life, why not write your own performance-evaluation notes?

These letters don't have to be fancy. One of my favorites was written by a lady who had set a goal to live within her clothing budget. She wrote herself the following letter, gave a friend twelve self-addressed, stamped envelopes, and asked him to mail one each month.

Dear Self:
OK, listen up! Pay attention! You promised to average $400 per month on clothing. Have you spent more than this so far this month? If so, STOP NOW.
Love, Me

As you grow in the process of accountability partnering, you will find more instances when you are capable of using yourself as the partner.

"We are what we repeatedly do. Excellence,
then, is not an act, but a habit."
—Aristotle

CHAPTER 20

THE POWER OF ACCOUNTABILITY

A woman who uses me as an accountability partner recently relayed the following story. A major focus of this woman's vision statement was to spend more one-on-one time with her daughter. If you have parented a teenager, then you know that your child (not you) determines when this kind of time will happen. One day, my friend was busy finishing a centerpiece for a dinner party. She was chastising herself for procrastinating the project when her youngest daughter walked in and said, "Mom, do you want to come with me to the mall?"

Initially, the mother wanted to respond, "I can't." She was focused on her task—trying to get it off her list. But then she remembered her new daughter-time goal, which led her to smile at her daughter, drop her project, and head to the mall. She later confessed that the prospect of sharing this story in a future accountability meeting had sparked this desire to act according to her vision.

As you experience this kind of direct link between your plans and your actions, you will internalize your goals and hence begin weaving your vision into your day-to-day life. In fact, many people have told me that they still remember how good they felt the first time they consciously followed their vision instead of simply responding to the issue immediately at hand. This leaves an indelible impression—a confidence in and appreciation for purposeful living.

With practice, momentum will build. In a reasonably short time, your goals will become ingrained in your daily decision-making process.

IMPLEMENTATION TOOL:
GOAL-DRIVEN DECISIONS

The next time you are working on minutiae tasks and an important goal offers itself for implementation (e.g., the above mall trip), just drop what you're doing and GO! Describe this occasion and its results in a reminder note to yourself. Reviewing this later will provide reinforcement and encouragement to inspire you to try it again and again until it becomes second nature.

> "It is only with the heart that one can see rightly;
> what is essential is invisible to the eye."
> —Antoine De Saint-Exupery

CHAPTER 21

THE SPIRITUAL FACTOR

Of all the ideas I will discuss in this book, the spiritual factor is the most powerful concept in terms of results.

Interestingly, this also seems to be the most sensitive and controversial issue. Since people react so positively to all the other concepts, you'd think I would choose to avoid the touchy subject of faith in God. But it would be unfair to omit this critical dimension.

Consider this example. You taste a marvelous food dish at a restaurant and ask the chef for the recipe. You're thrilled that he gives it to you, but when you try making it, the result doesn't taste quite like what you experienced at the restaurant. You go back to the chef and complain that it doesn't taste as good. He asks if you included all the ingredients and followed his preparation instructions, to which you respond, "I sure did, except I left out the meat." The chef rolls his eyes and says, "Then can't you guess why it didn't taste as good?"

Omitting the spiritual factor from purposeful living would be the equivalent of forgetting the meat in the recipe. Leave it out if you want to, but you'll be ignoring a major component.

This chapter applies to you no matter what your current faith, denomination, or beliefs are. And don't confuse "spiritual" with "religious." Spirituality deals with your relationship with your creator. Religion deals with human-made rules and organizations that outline how different groups interpret the appropriate expression of that relationship. In spiritual matters, we often spend too much time thinking about these man-made differences and too little time observing the effect of having God in our lives.

Consider oxygen. Picture yourself living before the existence of any scientific studies that form our current body of knowledge. I tell you that oxygen is in the air and is necessary to sustain life. You don't believe it; I can't prove it scientifically. But neither your disbelief nor my lack of evidence changes the fact that it exists and is critical to our survival.

I could go on to tell you that aerobic exercise will improve the effect that oxygen brings to your physical being. Given your incredulity about its very existence, you'd likely be a tough sell for a workout program. But you could certainly try jogging without changing your beliefs; you wouldn't have to reconsider your perspective if you didn't find that my suggestion helped you feel better.

I will be the first to admit that I haven't always been a huge proponent of exercise, nor of spirituality, for that matter. I lived the first half of my life without knowing God's presence. Sure, I had a vague sense of a supreme power that watched over me in times of trouble, so I would have told you I believed. But I didn't even have a hint of what it meant to receive continuous, day-to-day guidance from Him.

Since then, my appreciation for God's real power has grown exponentially as He has taken over more and more aspects of my life. The incredible thing about this process is that the more I grow in my relationship with God, the more I realize how much further I have to go. I'm convinced that it's limitless. So I can't tell you if I am 6 percent or 60 percent of the way to full realization. I can only tell you that you are not listening to an expert—I'm just a fellow traveler.

Don't assume that in sharing some detail of my own spiritual journey, I imply that this is the ideal route to a relationship with your creator. I simply pass on my story in order to encourage you to seek His plan for your life, whatever path you find. Remember, He's seeking you too.

As a prelude to the implementation steps below, I advise you to be honest. If you don't believe, tell God (He knows it anyway): "I don't believe, but I do strive to keep an open mind. If you're there, help me with my unbelief." And then listen with the knowledge that God's voice is not often the loudest in your life. He often opens and closes doors with a quiet click and trusts you to heed his suggestions.

IMPLEMENTATION TOOL: FINDING YOUR PATH

At the start of each day, spend quiet time in conversation with your God. Some like sitting still for this piece of time, while others prefer a brisk walk.

Regardless, early morning seems to be a great time to focus on His priorities for the coming day. Study God's word, and before each reading, simply ask Him to guide your understanding.

It helps to follow this with prayers of thanksgiving, confession, and concern for yourself and others.

Many people avoid prayer because they don't know the words. Forget it! Speak to God as if you were a child on your mother's knee. It's okay to say things like "I'm not sure if you are there," "I have a problem with my car," "I don't know how to love my enemy," or "I'm really scared about this problem." He doesn't want sophistication. He wants a relationship with you.

"I celebrate myself, and sing myself."
—Walt Whitman

CHAPTER 22

CELEBRATE

Did something great happen today? Congratulations! Did you stop your work, walk outside, shout out loud, smile, treat yourself to chocolate, and then go back to work? I hope so, but somehow I doubt it.

Most of us are quick to focus on what goes wrong—on what's missing. We are trained to focus on what went astray, to look at weak points instead of strengths. We forget to stop, reflect, and say, "Wow, that was really great!"

In the Old Testament of the Bible, marker stones were a tradition. When something memorable happened, people would often gather rocks and make a pile to commemorate the event. I think we can learn from that practice.

How did celebration depart from our lives? We hope for an event to happen, and later (often much later), when it finally happens as we wished, we don't stop to commemorate it. Furthermore, we don't write it down or record our feelings, and we therefore forget. In many ways, we don't even see it. And if meeting success isn't cause enough for celebration, how long can our motivation last?

IMPLEMENTATION TOOL: CHAMPAGNE

Keep a bottle of champagne on the top shelf of your refrigerator. Don't skimp; make it really nice stuff. Its top-shelf location will command your attention every day and help you reflect on whether you have cause to celebrate. And the fact that you've chosen such a nice bottle will remind you how valuable celebration is.

> "In creating, the only hard thing is to begin:
> a grass blade's no easier to make than an oak."
> —James Russell Lowell

CHAPTER 23

STARTING YOUR PLAN

Okay, you've thought through your vision and the various concepts that will help you accomplish it. So now you're ready to get into some specifics. When you're finished, you will have created a personal plan. This is the combination of your vision, which we covered earlier, and the goals that will lead you to your desired future picture.

Most people are exposed to planning through their jobs or committee meetings. Unfortunately, these experiences are typically exercises in numbers and predictable wording that we assemble into a notebook and leave to gather dust on a shelf.

Early in my career, I became accustomed to receiving a yearly letter (usually from the accounting department) stating that it was time to do "the plan." The memo would set a due date. All of us would start the process and begin planning. One year, a thought struck me: *Who is reminding me that my personal plan is due?* My answer was an immediate *nobody*.

Well, I'm here to tell you. YOUR PERSONAL PLAN IS DUE!

When my clients first sit down to actually write the goals in their plans, they often run into a mental block. They complain, "Gee, this all sounded good until I took pen and paper in hand, and then I just sat there!" I also hear, "I know I should do a plan, but it's such a huge and complex project … I just don't know where to start."

What these people are experiencing is the law of inertia. What we need to activate is the law of momentum.

Inertia was described earlier (a resting object stays at rest until acted on by an outside force). The law of momentum says that an object in motion will stay in motion until acted on by an outside force.

You've seen these laws at work when you start to push a loaded wheelbarrow. Getting it moving takes a burst of energy (you are overcoming inertia). Once you have it rolling, pushing it becomes easier because momentum takes over.

Now take this analogy and apply it to starting your personal plan. You need to get started to overcome inertia. Once you have it started, momentum will make it easier to move forward.

IMPLEMENTATION TOOL: GAINING MOMENTUM

Go back to the vision you developed in chapter four. Think about the key things you want to accomplish to make that future picture become a reality. This will be your preliminary list of goals. Carry it with you for several weeks while you add to it whenever a new objective comes to mind. During this period, don't screen out a single thought. Right now, your target is just quantity of ideas.

I once advised a young man who really took this seriously. His first list was terrific. It was two pages long and listed probably one hundred things he wanted to achieve in life. His goals ranged from "My children will grow up with a high self-image" all the way to "I'll have a job that allows me to bring my dog to work." That's exactly the idea—list absolutely every goal. Prioritizing will come later.

This is a helpful process. This data dump, often called brainstorming, is designed to get all your thoughts in front of you. You may end up with many similar entries. Such a pattern often reveals one of your high-priority goals.

Having done this list, you are beginning to overcome inertia … so let's not stop now or we'll lose momentum!

"If you have built castles in the air, your work need not be lost; that is where they should be. Now put the foundations under them."
—Henry David Thoreau

CHAPTER 24

CATEGORIZING YOUR GOALS

Some people initially struggle with the goal-listing process described in the prior chapter. If that's you, the goal categories listed here can help get you started.

At the same time, if you have already created a huge list, these categories will assist you in putting your goals into more manageable groupings.

If your items don't fit into the following list of categories, by all means add your own. This is simply a list of groupings that may help trigger ideas.

- Career
- Hobby
- Family
- Physical Health
- Spiritual Life
- Finances
- Self-Development
- Education
- Skill Enhancement
- Geographic Location
- Leisure Time
- Giving/Volunteering
- Mentoring

"The difference between a goal and a dream is the written word."
—Gene Donohue

CHAPTER 25

WORDING YOUR GOALS

At this point, you have a categorized list of goals. Now we're going to discuss how to review the wording of each goal to make certain that it passes the following tests.

Is it realistic? This does not mean "is it easy to achieve?" Rather, it means that you shouldn't create goals that are so extremely unlikely that you will end up ignoring them when you review them in the future. Some examples I've seen:

- "All my children will obey all our rules all the time."
- "I will always be happy."
- "I will never argue with my spouse."

Is it a means or an end? This can be subtle. You want to word your goals to state the desired result rather than the route to get there. Some examples are:

- "Win the lottery." In this case, the real goal was money, not how to get it.
- "Be in business for myself." Here, the actual goal turned out to be independence. For other people, it could have meant money, power, creativity, etc. In these cases, self-employment would be the means rather than the goal.

Is it measurable? Here's a very common trap. Many people define "measurable" as limited to numbers. This results in goals like, "I will exercise three days a week for twenty minutes each day." By the way, this is an okay goal, and it certainly is measurable. But don't limit all your goals to quantitative measurement. In my vocabulary, measurable simply means this: If you're honest with yourself, can you determine if you are achieving it? Numbers don't have to provide the only answer. Examples:

- "Create an atmosphere of teamwork on my church committee." While not quantifiable, high morale and lack of infighting will be obvious (and thereby measurable) to an astute observer.
- "Keep my family happy." This is not measurable because the true feelings of another person are too difficult to determine.
- "Exercise regularly." This is not measurable. What do you mean? How would you determine you had met this goal? You would need to add words to define "regularly."

Is it active or passive? Properly worded goals are active—you intend to act in ways to make them happen. Improper wording makes objectives passive—they're stated as a hope or wish.

- "I will stay healthy." This is a wish rather than a goal. Instead, focus on the things you can do for good health. Better goals would involve eating, exercise, and sleep habits that you want to change. These are things within your sphere of influence.
- "Have a mentor at work." This wording implies that it will just happen. Instead of this, set a goal to proactively cultivate a certain person as your guide, and then set sub-goals for how you will make this occur.

IMPLEMENTATION TOOL:
GOAL CHECK

After you re-word your goals per the above criteria, ask your accountability partner to review your statements. Without feedback, you are your only proofreader. This risks sloppy goal statements because, although you know what you meant to say today, in the future your memory may twist that original meaning so you fool yourself about your actual performance. Input from your accountability partner will help clarify and strengthen your goals.

"The rung of a ladder was never meant to rest upon, but only to hold a man's foot long enough to enable him to put the other somewhat higher."
—Thomas Henry Huxley

CHAPTER 26

PRIORITIZING YOUR GOALS

Now you are going to prioritize your goals. Remember that your preliminary list from the chapter "Starting Your Plan" holds every item that came to mind. Now it's time to decide each goal's importance in relation to the others.

Now here's a real challenge. Label each goal according to the following priority description.

PG: Primary Goal. Maximum of five goals.

- PGs are goals that are critical to the accomplishment of your vision. These go beyond worthwhile or important; they are indispensable. Without each being achieved, you believe a major part of your vision will go unrealized.

IG: Important Goal. Maximum of fifteen.

- IGs are very meaningful to you. You are willing to give them significant time and energy. They may contribute in some small part to your vision, but you realize that you can achieve it without these goals.

NG: Nice Goal. The rest of your goals.

- NGs are things you'd enjoy accomplishing. You want them on your final list, but you're willing to delay them or give them up when they compete with PGs or IGs.

For most people, this priority labeling is a very difficult step. The following exercise will assist you. It may help to have your accountability partner play the role of the magician.

IMPLEMENTATION TOOL: THE PRIORITIZING WAND

Pretend I have a magic wand. If I wave this wand, one goal on your list will be achieved for certain. However, if you choose this option, all your other goals are under higher risk. You may or may not achieve any of them. Which goal would you pick? Then, use the same process as if I said you could have two goals, then three, four, and finally five.

While you're doing this, you'll be saying "ouch" to yourself as you sacrifice certain goals in favor of your top five. Put a checkmark next to each "ouch." Those are the ones that you found very hard to put at risk.

When you're finished, go back over the whole list to confirm your choices or make changes.

At the end of this exercise, your top five goals are the PGs. Your checkmarks are your IGs (unless you have more than the allowed fifteen, in which case you have to decide which become NGs along with all your other remaining goals).

Most people like ranking much better than prioritizing. There is a huge difference between the two. Ranking allows you to think, "This is more important than that, but I will eventually do everything on the list. It's just a question of time." An example is your shopping list. You rank grocery store, dry cleaner, and hardware store. If you don't do them all today, you will do the others later.

In prioritizing, you have to consider that the other items on the list may be sacrificed—they may not be available at a later date. Let's look at the list in the above paragraph and reword it to say grocery store, dry cleaner, hardware store, and Susie's last soccer game. The last item cannot be done later.

This is how it works in life. Time is limited—it is a critical and nonrenewable resource. If you spend this immediate moment doing one thing, you can never use that spent time on something else. Don't fool yourself with ranking. Face the issue of prioritizing.

Don't read further until you have completed the magic wand tool above.

You haven't done the exercise and you're still reading? Well, you spoiled a little surprise.

If you desperately wanted to include just one more goal as a PG or just a couple more as IGs, that's okay. But forcing you to stay at a fixed number during the game—to make the really tough choices—is vital to developing meaningful priorities. Sure, you can go to six or seven PGs and to eighteen or twenty IGs. But only if you've first tried for five and fifteen respectively.

> "What lies behind us and what lies ahead of us are
> tiny matters compared to what lies within us."
> —Ralph Waldo Emerson

CHAPTER 27

YOUR PERSONAL
PLAN'S FINAL EXAM

Congratulations! You overcame inertia and kept the momentum going. You now have a written personal plan. It is your vision combined with the primary, important, and nice goals that will get you there.

IMPLEMENTATION TOOL:
EXAM TIME

Read your vision. Does it ignite your imagination? Can you picture it in details that make it real and personal?

Read your PGs (primary goals). Is each one independently critical to a major part of your vision?

Read your IGs (important goals). Were some of these hard to leave off your initial PG list? Is each one very important to you but not necessarily indispensable to your vision?

Read your NGs (nice goals). Do these include all of the stuff you'd enjoy doing but which are dispensable in comparison to the PGs and IGs?

If your answer to each question is yes, you are on your way forward … you have momentum.

If you answered any with no, some of the following common problems may help you diagnose and correct either your vision statement or your goals' priority designations.

If it's your vision statement that doesn't pass the test, the reason is probably that you worded it from your brain rather than your heart. Instead of dry, official language, try closing your eyes. Actually picture your future—sights, sounds, smells. Describe this image using your words rather than fancy phrases.

Maybe you have too many PGs, but each seems too indispensable to turn it into an IG. Sometimes a goal looks at first like a PG (critical to your vision) but it really isn't. For example, one American client's vision included a career helping Chinese and American corporations form joint ventures. At first, he had two of his PGs listed as:

- Learn the Chinese language.
- Form a consulting firm assisting with the formation of these ventures.

When he put these two through the final exam, the first goal passed the test—this skill would prove vital to his vision. But the second goal was actually an IG. In fact, he later ended up learning the language but giving up the consulting firm. Now he's still pursuing the vision, but from a job inside another company.

> "What we call the beginning is often the end. And to make an end is to make a beginning. The end is where we start from."
> —T.S. Eliot

FROM A READER'S PERSPECTIVE

When I sit down for a lunch meeting with my coach (the author of the very book you have just finished reading), he and I spend hours untangling the knots of my disorganized life. He listens to my babbling in typical Bill Munn fashion—sitting across the table with hands folded peacefully and every ounce of his concentration almost visibly wrapped around my disjointed monologue.

And when I finally run out of breath, he responds in typical Bill Munn fashion as well—hands working like visual highlighters across the text of his remarks. His observations are insightful, innovative, infuriating, and altogether true, and by the time we are packing up to go, I feel as though he has somehow reached across the table and replaced my backpack of stress with a bouquet of hopeful balloons. But before we reach the door, he stops me with one very simple question:

"So, exactly what are you going to do tomorrow in order to spark the changes we've discussed? What are the next steps you need to take in order to achieve your goals?"

Wow. Way to toss some sand in my balloons. I want to ask him if I can have just a moment to float inside of my reverie, but I know he's right. I know that while I babble on about my worries, he can sit across the table listening peacefully because he spends his days strolling inside of his vision. Perhaps that's why I feel closest to my own dreams when I'm with him.

But when I leave this coaching meeting, my next footstep will not automatically fall in the midst of the flourishing writing career that I have always dreamed of. Instead, my next footstep will fall directly in front of the last one, which, at the moment, happens to lead back to the lunch table where Bill and I haven't quite finished our meeting.

I pull my head out of the clouds and sit back down with my coach for a quick reality check. We discuss what I need to do tomorrow: contact a potential employer, assemble writing samples for an upcoming interview, research self-publishing. When I accomplish these small goals, I will not instantly become the best-selling author I hope to one day find in the mirror, but I will be a few steps closer to that goal, and I will have the advantage of momentum on my side.

With Bill as your coach, it is difficult to stand still and casually dream. He asks us all to live actively and intentionally—to use our ever-evolving vision as a sort-of road map to fulfillment. In the pages of this book, he has helped you begin the lifelong process of designing that map. Now it is up to you to take the next steps, kick your own momentum into motion, and begin living on purpose.

—Contributed by a client who wishes to remain anonymous

WANT TO GO DEEPER?

QUESTIONS for GROUP DISCUSSION

This discussion guide is included in response to feedback from readers who have decided to use Lead or Be Led as a tool to create group discussion.

Some readers have used the book for family discussions at the dinner table. Others communicated a desire to review the chapters at a book club. Some managers are using the material for staff sessions and management meetings to generate interchange and team building. Still other people are interested in group discussions in their volunteer organization meetings.

My coaching career has provided me many opportunities to observe individuals and groups as they verbalize their experiences and feelings around the subjects in the book. I hope these discussion ideas will assist you group in going deeper into the chapters and their applicability to people's lives.

As you proceed with your group, the following thoughts may help.

First, let people know they can "pass" on any question—they don't have to relate their feelings or experiences on that subject. Different people are in various stages of life at any point in time. Therefore, one may find a couple of chapters right on target for their current life experience while another responds to entirely different subjects. I encourage you to welcome this diversity of response as it will add richness to the group's interchange.

Secondly, if you think someone's answer is "off the subject" let it go. Correcting them may shut them down from addressing future topics. Also, what you consider a diversion from the issue may trigger a discussion that brings out matters that the group has positive energy about pursuing. When they're finished, simply repeat the discussion question to steer the conversation back on course.

Thirdly, agree to keep discussions confidential within the group.

Another hint is for the group to read the next meeting's question(s) so they can review the chapter and think about their response, if any.

PROLOGUE—The Trip

Group Discussion Topics:

(1) Re-read the prologue and try to personally climb into the story and picture yourself as a participant. Discuss any parts of Ted or Carol's thoughts or dialogue which are relevant to your own experience.

(2) Talk with the group about your personal experience with "exit ramps" on your life journey to-date.

Following are the group discussion topics suggested for each chapter.

Chapter 1 ONLY THREE LIVES CHANGED

(1) Give an example of a time you strongly desired to change a behavior but the project looked so large that the lack of an immediate next step, or implementation tool, resulted in your never tackling the issue.

(2) Share an experience where you were like the friend in the story who needed exercise and you were successful because you started with small next steps.

Chapter 2 LEAD or BE LED

(1) Toward the end of this chapter read the examples of people reacting to Ted and Carol's experience (e.g. "I know I should plan but..."). Which of these examples resonate with you personally? What other examples of your own reactions would fit these same themes?

Chapter 3 MEET YOUR ENEMY

(1) Share with the group an example where you or someone else used "as soon as" or "if only" as an explanation or excuse for not proceeding to act on a goal. *LEADER: Write these on a flip chart as people bring them up so you can see how many you can add to the list of examples at the beginning of the chapter.*

Chapter 4 THE POWER OF YOUR VISION

(1) Give an example of a vision, mission, or purpose statement you considered empty, phony, or meaningless to you. Is there an example of one that inspired you?

(2) In #1 above, if there was a statement that inspired you, what components did it have that you think resulted in this positive reaction?

(3) Picture the Implementation Tool moment when "Bill opens his briefcase..." What 1-3 key things do you know you want to be true of your life in the future?

Chapter 5 THE CIRCLE of LIFE

(1) Many people picture retirement as a time to coast. If, instead, you envision "finishing well" in your later years, what priority ingredients does that definition hold for you personally.

(2) How would you describe where you are now in the Circle of Life?

(3) Describe an experience where you mentored someone or you were mentored by someone else. How did it affect you? What was its value?

Chapter 6 MASTER YOUR DO LIST

(1) Discuss your reaction to the irony of how we view (non-renewable) time versus how we treat (renewable) money.

(2) Describe the situation if you have experienced doing non-priority stuff just to get them off the Do List so you don't have to rewrite them to a new sheet?

(3) If you prefer a paper-based system versus electronic, please discuss your reasons and your level of willingness to consider electronic.

Chapter 7 TAME the MONSTERS

(1) Is there one monster project which you could commit right now to breaking down into manageable pieces?

Chapter 8 APPOINTMENTS with YOURSELF

(1) What do you picture as your personal venues for appointments with yourself: Lunch? A walk in the park? Coffee house? Others? Think about all the choices that appeal to you.

(2) If you thought this concept would be a help to you, discuss the type of project you'd use at the beginning to "take to lunch." What would be the initial frequency of your appointments?

(3) Which of you would like to commit to trying an appointment with yourself before the next meeting date and report your experience back to the group?

Chapter 9 THE RIPENING of a PROBLEM

(1) Share with the group a story of a problem you tried to solve before it was ripe. Especially note in hind sight, now that you've been introduced to ripening, symptoms about this problem that you'd now look for to tell you the issue wasn't ready to be solved.

(2) Tell your story of a problem you once thought needed solving, was not resolved, and it turn out not to need resolution. In short, it never did become ripe.

Chapter 10 FORGET ABOUT JOBS

(1) Analyze your current function from the perspective of the recommended "goals versus tasks" highlighted in the story of the Billing Services Representative. How would you re-title your current role to emphasize the real goals of the position from the perspective of an owner? For example, the Billing Services Representative in our story might be re-titled "Receiver of Customer Input which The Organization Uses to Add Customer Perceived Value to Our Service."

(2) Are people in your organization focused more on the broader objectives or more on "that's not my job?" What could management do to broaden peoples' perspective? What could operational people do? What could YOU do to help this process?

Chapter 11 FIND YOUR POWER ALLEY

(1) What attribute have you most often heard from people, "Oh, that's you!"?

(2) Would you be interested in committing to the group that you'll take the next month to pursue the Implementation Tool in this chapter and report back to the group the results of this Attributes Analysis?

Chapter 12 WHAT ABOUT WEAKNESSES?

(1) Think through, and talk to the group about, the Implementation Tool at the end of the chapter and list your strategy to address your key weaknesses under the categories of balance, soften, or ignore.

(2) What "opposite person" could you enlist for the "balance" attributes?

(3) What baby steps would you find easiest to do to address the "soften" items?

(4) What weakness have people been most consistent in trying to get you to fix? How successful have these efforts been? Would you be comfortable just trying to drop these efforts—to let it go?

(5) Give an example of a "weakness moment"—a time when your awareness of your own weakness helped you (with the assistance of another person's strength) come to a solution space.

Chapter 13 EDUCATION

(1) Read the list of skills and mental disciplines (love of learning, etc.) and pick up to 3 subjects which you'd be most interested working on even if no one knew you were doing it or gave you any credit or income for doing so. Feel free to add other subjects not in the chapter's list.

(2) When was the last time you pursued something new, took a class, or explored a topic that interested you? Describe how it felt. Were you energized, challenged, etc.?

Chapter 14 FINANCIAL COMPENSATION

(1) Describe the behavior of people (names not required) you have known or with whom you've worked whose actions indicated they did not understand the long term relationship between their compensation and the value they deliver.

(2) Think about someone you know who does not understand that their long term financial compensation is determined by the value they deliver. What could you say or do that would begin to enlighten such an individual?

Chapter 15 WHAT DO YOU WANT TO DO?

(1) Describe the top 1-3 items on your "Love List" and your "Dread List."

(2) What ideas do you have about how you could include more "Love" items, or omit "Dread" items from your current occupation?

Chapter 16 FAIL FAST and FORWARD

(1) Describe a decision you made even though you only had a small portion of the information you wish you had. In hindsight, did you exaggerate your need for more facts? Would the results have been worse or better if you'd waited to decide?

(2) As you read the "2 foot deep lake" example of evaluating the cost of failure, did it remind you of any decisions you've made where you would have fretted less if you had analyzed the cost of failure to be relatively small?

(3) Risk tolerant people are comfortable with decisive action and failing fast and forward. Risk averse people do not like decisions and often analyze at length. What life experiences do you think influence how an adult falls on this continuum?

(4) What examples can you add to the list of so called "failures" at the end of the chapter?

Chapter 17 GIVING

(1) Whatever your attitude toward giving, share with the group how you think you learned this view? For example, it could have been experiences, the influence of an admired role model, training, etc.

(2) Relate a story of how your own receipt of the generosity of others affected your own thoughts about giving.

(3) Have you witnessed someone (including yourself?) move from an anti-giving attitude to a generous approach? If so, what changes seemed to occur in the person?

(4) What's the difference in giving when it's done with no thought of reciprocation versus when the donor expects something in return?

Chapters 18-20 ACCOUNTABILITY

(1) Discuss your reaction to the idea of inviting another person to be your accountability partner. What positives do you feel? What negatives? What areas do you question but haven't concluded yet?

(2) Which people can you picture inviting as partners depending on the goal you are setting? What traits did you look for in these people as you formed this list?

(3) Write a self-accountability note to yourself that you would have a partner mail to you in a few months. Share it with the group.

(4) Working together with the group, list the reasons accountability (self and partnering) is such a powerful tool in achieving goals.

(5) If you were asked to be someone else's accountability partner, what behaviors by that person would add to your motivation and your ability to help that person?

(6) As you look back over your life, even if you were not conscious of the accountability concept, can you recall a time where someone was your accountability partner? Describe the impact and how it worked.

Chapters 21 THE SPIRITUAL FACTOR

(1) The chapter begins with the observation that spiritual issues are often sensitive and controversial. Why do you think this is true?

(2) An early saint reportedly observed that there is a God-shaped void in each of us that is yearning to be filled. Discuss your reaction to this observation: agree/disagree? Experiences with this "void"?

(3) Share with the group your spiritual journey to date. Where are you now? Where do you feel you're going?

(4) Many of us were taught that prayer should follow certain "rules" regarding words to use, places to pray, voice tone, etc. The book talks about a more conversational tone, praying in your own words and saying exactly what you feel. Relate to the group your experiences with, and reaction to, these two approaches to prayer.

(5) The chapter discusses the "oxygen analogy" suggesting that our inability to see, prove, or explain something does not mean it isn't real and doesn't affect our lives. See if your group discussion can unveil examples. For example, it's a mystery how birds migrate on time and accurately across huge distances.

(6) There is an ancient tradition called "examen." You may want to try this privately whether or not you care to share the results with the group. Examen works like this. Each day you think through yesterday with an eye toward seeing where God was at work in your life. This could be as major as miraculous healing or as simple as admiring the perfection of a flower petal. Would you care to share with the group any of these moments from your recent past?

Chapters 22 CELEBRATE

(1) Most people receive "report cards" regularly. This may come in the form of a test grade, comment from a customer, review from a boss, a comment from a friend, or input from a family member. Many of us quickly skip over the "A" grades (with short—or zero—celebration) and dwell at length on the "D's and F's" Are you (or someone you know) like this? What do you think are the reasons you (or they) downplay the celebration?

(2) Looking at this past week, list each positive event that has occurred. Next to each item, indicate if and how you celebrated.

Chapters 23-24 STARTING YOUR PLAN & CATEGORIZING YOUR GOALS

(1) Share with each other some of the inertia challenges you've had in getting started with your plan.

(2) Practice the implementation tool at the end of chapter 23 wherein you begin listing everything that comes to your mind as a potential component of your plan. Discuss with the group how this worked for you? Did it help you jump start the process?

(3) Relate to the group other inertia-conquering ideas you've found helpful—either in this planning process or in any other challenge you've faced in getting started with a major effort.

(4) As a group, go through the categories of goals in chapter 24. Which ones were areas you might have otherwise overlooked? What additional categories are not listed which are relevant to your vision?

Chapters 25 WORDING YOUR GOALS

(1) Give to the group examples of goals you had originally written in such a way that they were "unrealistic".

(2) Discuss up to 3 goal ideas (from chapter 23) which may be worded as "means" versus "ends" and help each other re-word those.

(3) Talk about examples of goals you have which you believe to be measurable, while they may not be quantifiable.

(4) Share with the group goals you initially had worded in such a way that they were "passive" instead of "active" and how you re-phrased them to be active.

Chapters 26 PRIORITIZING YOUR GOALS

(1) Relate to your team up to 3 examples of those of your goals that fall into each of the three categories: Priority, Important, and Nice.

(2) Discuss your reaction to the difference between "ranking" and "prioritizing" which is covered in the implementation tool. Give examples from your own experience where this may have helped you clarify the difference between two.

Chapters 27 YOUR PERSONAL PLAN'S FINAL EXAM

(1) Share with the group a few of your vision components which you're having trouble wording in such a way that they capture your heart instead of just your brain.

(2) Show examples of vision components where you successfully re-worded the statement from brain-based to heart-engaging.

Chapters 28 LET YOUR PLAN LIVE

(1) Brainstorm with your group any methods you can think of which will help you keep your vision and plan in front of you—on your radar screen—on a regular basis.

(2) The book recommends keeping your plan flexible but not going so far with this that you find yourself changing it on a whim. As you think about this balance between the two, in which direction do you think you are most likely to fault—too rigid or constantly changing direction?

IN CLOSING ….. A REQUEST

Please share with me discussion topic ideas which occurred to you during this process. Simply go to leadorbeled.net where you will find a box to contact me. Then write in your idea plus which chapter it fits. Thank you for your intentionality!

Bill Munn

ABOUT THE AUTHOR

Bill Munn has made a career of helping others live on purpose.

After receiving his MBA and working as a professor of finance and economics, he transitioned into the corporate world, where he spent twenty years in management and developed a talent for helping his colleagues achieve their goals.

Fifteen years ago, Bill decided to live out his passion by sharing his innovative and open-minded approach to business and life management. Since forming his own coaching company, his clients have included corporate presidents, management executives, entrepreneurs, business owners, church leaders, and individuals making career decisions.

He and his wife, Lindy, split their time between Ohio and beautiful Northern Michigan, where they often welcome their three daughters, two sons-in-law, and six grandchildren into their empty nest. *Lead or Be Led* is Bill's first book.

If you would like to contact Bill regarding his seminars and personal coaching sessions, please send an e-mail to billmunn@leadorbeled.net.

Printed in the United States
132552LV00002BA/2/P